TOOLS FOR CAREGIVERS

- **F&P LEVEL:** A
- **WORD COUNT:** 29

- **CURRICULUM CONNECTIONS:**
  animals, community

Skills to Teach

- **HIGH-FREQUENCY WORDS:** a, I, see
- **CONTENT WORDS:** fish, frog, jellyfish, panda, snake, tiger, zookeeper
- **PUNCTUATION:** exclamation points
- **WORD STUDY:** compound words (*jellyfish, zookeeper*); long /a/, spelled a (*snake*); long /e/, spelled ee (*see, zookeeper*); long /i/, spelled, i (*tiger*); /oo/, spelled oo (*zoo, zookeeper*); short /a/, spelled a (*panda*); short /i/, spelled i (*fish, jellyfish*); short /o/, spelled o (*frog*)
- **TEXT TYPE:** factual description

Before Reading Activities

- Read the title and give a simple statement of the main idea.
- Have students "walk" though the book and talk about what they see in the pictures.
- Introduce new vocabulary by having students predict the first letter and locate the word in the text.
- Discuss any unfamiliar concepts that are in the text.

After Reading Activities

Ask readers if they have been to the zoo. What was their favorite animal? If they haven't been, ask them to think about an animal they would like to see. Have each student draw that animal and show his or her picture to the class. Ask them to explain what the animal is and either why it was their favorite animal at the zoo or why they would want to see this animal at the zoo.

Tadpole Books are published by Jump!, 5357 Penn Avenue South, Minneapolis, MN 55419, www.jumplibrary.com

Copyright ©2021 Jump. International copyright reserved in all countries. No part of this book may be reproduced in any form without written permission from the publisher.

Editor: Jenna Gleisner **Designer:** Michelle Sonnek

Photo Credits: Vaclav Volrab/Shutterstock, cover (left); Nejron Photo/Shutterstock, cover (right); Eric Isselee/Shutterstock, 1, 2mr, 6–7; ImageSource/iStock, 2tl, 3 (kids); Grigorev Mikhail/Shutterstock, 2tl, 3 (fish); Rodney Gardie/Shutterstock, 4–5; SebastiaanPeeters/Shutterstock, 2ml, 8–9; Zeedoherty/Shutterstock, 2bl, 10–11; Blue Jean Images/Alamy, 2tr, 12–13; Tiffany Bryant/Shutterstock, 2br, 14–15; Oleg Znamenskiy/Shutterstock, 16.

Library of Congress Cataloging-in-Publication Data
Names: Zimmerman, Adeline J., author.
Title: Zoo / by Adeline J. Zimmerman.
Description: Tadpole book edition. | Minneapolis: Jump!, Inc., (2021) | Series: Around town | Includes index. | Audience: Ages 3–6
Identifiers: LCCN 2019047621 (print) | LCCN 2019047622 (ebook) | ISBN 9781645274803 (hardcover) | ISBN 9781645274810 (paperback) | ISBN 9781645274827 (ebook)
Subjects: LCSH: Zoos—Juvenile literature.
Classification: LCC QL76 .Z56 2021 (print) | LCC QL76 (ebook) | DDC 590.73—dc23
LC record available at https://lccn.loc.gov/2019047621
LC ebook record available at https://lccn.loc.gov/2019047622

AROUND TOWN

ZOO

by Adeline J. Zimmerman

TABLE OF CONTENTS

tadpole books

WORDS TO KNOW

fish

jellyfish

panda

snake

tiger

zookeeper

ZOO

I see a fish!

frog · · · · ▷

I see a frog!

snake

I see a snake!

panda ·····▶

I see a panda!

tiger

I see a tiger!

jellyfish

I see a jellyfish!

zookeeper ·····▶

owl

I see a zookeeper!

LET'S REVIEW!

What zoo animal is this?

INDEX